Extreme Aircraft!

Q&A

Smithsonian | Collins

An Imprint of HarperCollinsPublishers

WHITE KNIGHT

Smithsonian Mission Statement

For more than 160 years, the Smithsonian has remained true to its mission, "the increase and diffusion of knowledge." Today the Smithsonian is not only the world's largest provider of museum experiences supported by authoritative scholarship in science, history, and the arts, but also an international leader in scientific research and exploration. The Smithsonian offers the world a picture of America, and America a picture of the world.

Special thanks to Peter Jakab, Curator, National Air and Space Museum, Smithsonian Institution, for his invaluable contribution to this book.

This book was created by **jacob packaged goods LLC** (www.jpgglobal.com).
Written by: Sarah L. Thomson
Creative: Ellen Jacob, Kirk Cheyfitz, Carolyn Jackson, Sherry Williams, Jeff Chandler, Brenda Murray

Photo credits: title page: © Mike Mills/Scaled Composites; **page 3:** top: Smithsonian SI-85-11071~P; bottom: APImages; **page 4, inset:** Lilienthal jumping with viewers: Smithsonian NASM 73-2249; **pages 4–5:** Smithsonian SI-87-17029~Q; **page 5, inset:** Cayley glider drawings: Smithsonian NASM 85-18307; **page 6:** Smithsonian SI A-4691; **page 7:** Library of Congress; **page 8, inset:** Smithsonian NASM SI Neg. No. 73-05535; **pages 8–9:** Smithsonian XRA-6761~P; **page 10, inset left:** page 1 of letter: Smithsonian 210-L3-S3bh; **inset center:** watch: Smithsonian; **inset right:** page 2 of letter: Smithsonian 210-L3-S3ah; **pages 10–11:** Smithsonian SI-A-26767-B~Q; **page 12:** U.S. Air Force 021009-O-9999G-003; **page 13:** U.S. Air Force 051011-F-0000R-001; **page 14, inset:** Courtesy of Special Collections and Archives, Wright State University, WR6G6; **pages 14–15:** U.S. Air Force 020925-F-9999s-0029; **page 15, inset:** Imagine That! Design; **page 16, inset:** Smithsonian SI-93-7758~P; **pages 16–17:** Smithsonian NASM SIA-4463; **pages 18–19:** © Mike Oniffrey; **page 19, inset:** © Mike Oniffrey; **page 20, inset:** Smithsonian SI-98-20490~P; **pages 20–21:** © Boeing Management Company; **page 21 inset:** James Doolittle: Smithsonian SI-2003-7~P; **page 22, inset:** Smithsonian SI-76-13317~P; **pages 22–23:** Smithsonian SI-85-11071~P; **page 25:** U.S. Air Force 050317-F-1234P-034; **pages 26–27:** Smithsonian SI-84-10658~P; **page 27, inset:** Department of Defense DA-SD-03-06520; **page 28, inset:** Smithsonian SI-97-17485~P; **pages 28–29:** Smithsonian 99-41036.7; **page 29, inset:** APImages; **page 30, inset:** U.S. Air Force 020905-o-9999g-010; **pages 30–31:** APImages; **pages 32–33:** top: APImages; bottom: © BAE SYSTEMS; **page 34:** courtesy Airbus; **page 35:** APImages; **pages 36–37:** NASA; **page 39:** NASA GPN-2000-001031; inset: Smithsonian SI-2001-2277~P; **pages 40–41:** © Mike Mills/Scaled Composites; **page 41, inset:** APImages; **page 42:** top: Library of Congress; center: Smithsonian SI-A-26767-B~Q; bottom: © Mike Oniffrey; **page 43:** top: © Boeing Management Company; center: Smithsonian SI-97-17485~P; bottom: APImages; **page 45:** Carolyn Russo, National Air and Space Museum, Smithsonian Institution; **page 46:** courtesy Airbus; **page 47:** top: Smithsonian SI 84-10658~P; bottom: Smithsonian 99-41036.7.

Contents

Who had the first idea for a flying machine?

Long before jets and helicopters and spaceships, people dreamed about flight.

Courageous Otto Lilienthal made more than 2,000 glider flights. (Inset) In 1892, Lilienthal launches one of his gliders by running and jumping off a hilltop.

More than 500 years ago, an artist in Italy named **Leonardo da Vinci** drew plans for flying machines. But as far as we know, he never actually built one.

Three hundred years later, Sir George Cayley of England did build a flying machine, with wings that spread wide to float on the wind. This type of aircraft is called a **glider.** Cayley built small gliders at first, then later made ones big enough to carry a person. He even had his stable boy fly in one of them. Otto Lilienthal of Germany also experimented with flight. He strapped on his glider, ran to the edge of a hill, and jumped off. Then he floated through the air, sometimes for close to a quarter mile.

Sir George Cayley drew detailed designs for his gliders.

Cayley and Lilienthal had found one way to fly.

But even before gliders, people had experimented with another kind of flight.

SMITHSONIAN LINK
Learn all about early flight, including the Lilienthal Hang Glider, at:
http://www.nasm.si.edu/exhibitions/gal107/gal107.html

How does a balloon fly?

A balloon will fly if the gas inside is lighter than the air around it. It can be filled with hot air that is lighter than the cooler air outside it. Or it can be filled with a light gas such as **hydrogen.** Either way, the balloon will float up, carrying people beneath it. This kind of flying is called lighter-than-air flight.

In 1783, Joseph and Étienne Montgolfier of France built the first successful hot-air balloon. Its passengers were a duck, a rooster, and a sheep. One of the people watching said the animals were "much astonished." Later the same year, two men soared aloft in a similar balloon made by the Montgolfier brothers, becoming the first humans to make a lighter-than-air flight with no connection to the ground.

The first flight sending humans into the air was on this Montgolfier brothers' balloon that rose above a park in Paris.

Although balloons can fly high in the air, they are hard to control.

There is no way to make a balloon change direction. People began trying to figure out how to make a balloon they could steer.

A balloon is simply a big bag full of hot air or another kind of gas.

This painting shows Jac Charles and Noel Robert flying their balloon over Paris on December 1, 1783.

What is an airship, or a dirigible?

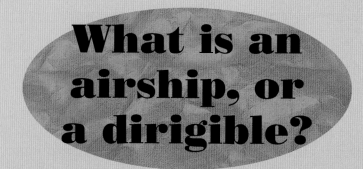

An airship is a large balloon with an engine and a **propeller** to move it forward. It also has a tail, which enables the ship to turn or go up and down. Because airships were the first flying machines that could change direction in midair, they are sometimes called dirigibles, which comes from a Latin word that means "to steer."

Henri Giffard of France made the first successful airship flight. He attached a small steam engine to a cigar-shaped balloon and flew for 17 miles. A few years later, Alberto Santos-Dumont used more powerful engines in his airships.

Henri Giffard flew the first airship in 1852.

The dirigible *Hindenburg* made ten transatlantic flights before exploding over New Jersey.

The **Hindenburg,** one of the largest airships ever built, could carry **72 passengers.**

In one of his famous flights, he circled the Eiffel Tower in Paris in 1903.

During the 1920s and 1930s, airships became bigger and faster and were soon a popular way to travel. The *Hindenburg* could fly at about 80 miles an hour. But a year after its first flight, the hydrogen gas inside the giant airship caught fire. Thirty-six people were killed.

After the *Hindenburg* disaster, airships became less and less popular and were no longer used to carry many passengers. Another invention was becoming more important—the **airplane.**

SMITHSONIAN LINK
Want to learn more about the science behind flight? Visit the "How Things Fly" exhibition in the National Air and Space Museum.
http://www.nasm.si.edu/exhibitions/gal109/gal109.html

Who flew the first plane with an engine?

In 1899, Wilbur Wright wrote a letter to the Smithsonian asking for information about flying. Less than four years later, he timed his brother Orville's first flight with this stopwatch.

On a windy day in December 1903, Orville and Wilbur Wright went to a beach near Kitty Hawk, North Carolina, to test their new flying machine. They called it, simply, the Flyer. The two brothers shook hands and Orville climbed aboard. The Flyer moved slowly down a wooden track and then lifted into the air. Orville was flying! The flight didn't last long—only 12 seconds.

Orville flew 120 feet, about half the length of a football field.

The Wright brothers made three more flights that same day. On the last, Wilbur flew 852 feet in 59 seconds.

The Flyer was heavier-than-air, unlike a balloon or an airship. In contrast to a glider, it had an engine so it could move under its own power. It was the first real airplane. Soon there would be more.

SMITHSONIAN LINK
Check out the National Air and Space Museum's "The Wright Brothers & The Invention of the Aerial Age" online exhibit.
http://www.nasm.si.edu/wrightbrothers/

Wilbur Wright watches as his brother Orville pilots their famous Flyer on its first successful flight.

How many wings did the first planes have?

During the early years of flying, many planes had two sets of wings, just as the Flyer did. This type of aircraft is called a biplane. ("Bi" means "two.") Some planes even had three sets of wings. Planes with more than one set of wings were slow but sturdy.

A few early pilots flew monoplanes with one set of wings. ("Mono" means "one.") The first monoplanes were fast but fragile.

Colonel H. M. Hickam, an early leader in building what became the U.S. Air Force, stands in front of an experimental military biplane—the S.E. 5—in 1920.

What were these planes made of?

People tried to make these early planes as light as possible so it would be easier to get them airborne. They made the planes out of wood, cloth, and wire— the lightest materials they had.

With one set of wings or two or three, all these planes still got up into the air. How did they manage to stay there?

SMITHSONIAN LINK
Visit the National Air and Space Museum's new exhibit called "America by Air."
http://www.nasm.si.edu/exhibitions/gal102/americabyair/

The only exact replica of one of the world's most famous biplanes, the Wright brothers' 1905 Flyer, flies over the brothers' home airfield in Ohio.

What makes an airplane stay up?

We usually think of air as nothing. But air can actually be very powerful. (Think of the wind power of hurricanes and tornadoes.)

The curved wings with movable flaps of this C-141 Starlifter jet allow it to make banked turns.

Wilbur Wright twisted, or warped, the wings of the Flyer for the same purpose.

LIFT

Flight Direction

Low pressure, faster airflow

High pressure, slower airflow

Modern wing shapes are more streamlined than the Wright brothers' design, but they use the same principles.

Air pushing against objects makes a force called air pressure. Air pressure can create **lift**, which may be strong enough to overcome **gravity**, the force that keeps airplanes—and everything else—down on the ground.

Lift is created when air flows over an airplane's wings. The wing is curved so that air flowing over the top moves more quickly than air flowing under the bottom. The slower air underneath the wing creates greater pressure than the faster air above it, and the plane is pushed up into the sky.

In order to take off, a plane races down a runway. The forward motion of the speeding plane is called **thrust**. Thrust has to be strong enough to overcome another force—**drag**. Drag is air pushing back against an object that tries to move. Planes are very streamlined, or smooth. This is so air flows over them as easily as possible to create less drag.

Gravity pulls a plane down, but lift pushes it up.

Thrust moves a plane forward, but drag slows it down. If lift is stronger than gravity, and thrust is stronger than drag, the plane will fly.

Popular African American barnstormer Bessie Coleman had to learn to fly in France.

Pilots wanted to race, to do stunts, and to show off how well they could fly.

Daredevil Gladys Ingle prepares to make a midair transfer from the upper right wing of one airplane to the lower left wing of another plane.

What was a barnstormer?

Less than 10 years after the Wright brothers' first flight, some pilots weren't satisfied just to get a plane up in the air. By the 1920s, these daredevil pilots were called barnstormers. They flew upside down or looped the loop. A passenger sometimes walked out on the wing or did parachute jumps.

By the 1930s, airplane races had become a popular sport.

Thousands of fans watched events such as the National Air Races. To compete, pilots wanted the fastest planes they could get, so builders tried new ideas to make planes quicker and more powerful.

The Gee Bee was a racing plane designed for speed. It had the smallest possible frame built around the biggest possible engine. Gee Bees thrilled air-racing fans. And some of those fans became something else—passengers.

What plane was the first modern airliner?

Radial motors still power this restored Ford Tri-Motor.

Bigger planes were built to take passengers from place to place. The first U.S. passenger plane made completely of metal, the Ford Tri-Motor, was completed in 1926, in the middle of the barnstorming era. Different models of the Tri-Motor could carry from 8 to 17 people. It was nicknamed the "Tin Goose," even though it wasn't really made of tin. It was actually made of aluminum. One engine and propeller were located on the plane's nose, and the other two were on the wings.

New, more comfortable all-metal airplanes replaced the Tri-Motor. The Boeing 247 is considered the first modern passenger plane, or airliner. It had one engine on each wing, which gave 10 passengers a smooth, quiet ride at 160 miles per hour. After takeoff, its wheels folded up into the wings, helping the plane soar smoothly through the air.

The small, sturdy Douglas DC-3 first entered service in 1936 and became very familiar

SMITHSONIAN LINK
Read more about the history of air transportation and some of the first passenger planes, including the Ford Tri-Motor, at:
http://www.nasm.si.edu/exhibitions/gal102/gal102.html#trimot

Tri-Motor passengers relaxed in heavily padded metal seats.

to passengers in the early days of air travel. At one time, 9 out of every 10 passengers in a plane flew in a DC-3 or a smaller version, the DC-2. Ten thousand DC-3s were made in 11 years, and some are still flying today. A DC-3 could carry 21 passengers and reach 230 miles per hour.

Two powerful engines, one on each wing, helped the plane fly easily with a heavy load or in bad weather.

Airliners took people from city to city, landing at busy airports. But some places had no airports. New planes were designed to reach them.

What is a seaplane?
What is a flying boat?

The big flying boats, such as this Boeing 314 Clipper from 1938, were the most popular passenger planes of the 1930s.

Pan American Airways advertised some of the routes of its giant flying boats in this poster.

PAN AMERICAN AIRWAYS SYSTEM

Cuba-Mexico
West Indies
Central and
South America

SAVES TWO DAYS OUT OF THREE · PASSENGERS · AIRMAIL · EXPRESS

People felt safe crossing the ocean in these planes, knowing that they wouldn't sink.

A seaplane doesn't need a runway. Instead, it takes off and lands on water. It has floats under its wings instead of wheels, so it can rest on top of the water.

Giant aircraft called flying boats were the most popular passenger planes in the 1930s. Flying boats didn't have floats under their wings. Instead, the body of the plane was shaped like a boat and could float.

The Boeing 314 Clipper was the biggest flying boat ever made and the largest passenger plane in the world for 30 years. Like a flying hotel, it had a dining room, kitchen, lounge, and sleeping berths. With a top speed of 192 miles per hour, the Clipper could carry 74 passengers across the Atlantic and to other faraway places.

Planes let people travel more quickly and easily than they ever had before. But travel wasn't the only use people found for airplanes.

James Doolittle, a famous aviation pioneer in the U.S. Army Air Corps, stands on one float of a seaplane, the Curtiss R3C-2 Racer.

When were airplanes first used in war?

Two global wars—World War I (1914–1918) and World War II (1939–1945)—were fought in the first half of the twentieth century. Both sides discovered new uses for airplanes.

Mounting a machine gun on a plane turned it into a weapon. It was dangerous work flying fighter planes such as the German Fokker Dr. I triplane or the British Sopwith Camel in the First World War. The cockpit, where the pilot sat, was open to the wind and cold. The planes were made of wood and cloth, and they burned easily. Even so, young men flew in daring battles, called dogfights, to shoot down enemy planes.

In World War I, German Baron Manfred von Richthofen shot down 80 enemy planes in his famous red planes to earn the nickname the "Red Baron."

The British-made Sopwith Camel helped the Allies take back the skies over Europe from the Germans.

By World War II, fighter planes were now made of metal. Many could fly around 400 miles per hour. Spitfires, each carrying eight machine guns, helped to defend British troops at **Dunkirk** as they retreated from France. Planes also bombed targets on the ground. At first, pilots leaned out of their cockpits to drop bombs by hand. Later, heavier planes called bombers carried explosives under their wings or inside the body of the plane. The U.S. B-29, flown in World War II, was called the Super-fortress because of all the bombs it could carry—20,000 pounds of them.

SMITHSONIAN LINK
Learn about the warplanes of the Great War at:
http://www.nasm.si.edu/exhibitions/gal206/gal206.html

Helicopters are great for water rescues every day and at war.

How does a helicopter fly?

People use planes for stunts and races, to carry passengers and **cargo,** and to fight wars. But planes can't go everywhere.

Airplanes have long wings out to the sides. Helicopters have spinning blades called rotors on top. As the rotor blades spin, they act like wings and create lift to carry the helicopter up into the sky.

Along with all their advantages, helicopters have one big limitation. Because of the way the rotors work, no helicopter can fly faster than about 250 miles an hour.

What can helicopters do that planes can't?

Many people experimented with helicopters. Leonardo da Vinci drew plans for one. But the first person to design and build a successful helicopter was Igor Sikorsky. Early helicopters tended to spin out of control and crash. Sikorsky's VS-300 helicopter had a small rotor on its tail that kept it balanced.

A plane needs a long, flat surface to take off from and to land on. A helicopter can land in a small space. It can hover like a hummingbird, move straight up or down, and even fly backward.

As helicopters were being developed, people were also experimenting with a faster kind of airplane—a jet.

Helicopters were first used for rescue by the U.S. military in the Korean War.

How does a jet engine work?

Early airplanes had engines that turned propellers to move the planes forward. But a new kind of engine created a new kind of plane—a jet. A jet engine sucks in air, which is compressed, or forced, into a tiny space and mixed with **jet fuel,** which is ignited. The burning fuel heats the air, and the hot air bursts out of the engine and forces the plane forward much faster than a propeller could.

Jets have streamlined shapes so they can move smoothly through the air. Like a shark, which can swim quickly through water, jets have long, cone-shaped noses at the front and smooth bodies with nothing to catch the wind. Jets also have thin wings pointed toward the rear of the plane.

Less than 50 years after Orville and Wilbur got the Flyer into the air, an airplane actually flew faster than the speed of sound.

NASA's X-43A scramjet reached a speed almost ten times the speed of sound in 2004.

SMITHSONIAN LINK
See which aircraft engines are currently on display at the Steven F. Udvar-Hazy Center:
http://www.nasm.si.edu/museum/udvarhazy/artifacts_engines.cfm

The world's first jet plane, a German Heinkel He 178, reached a speed of 400 miles per hour in 1939.

Air Force One is actually two different Boeing 747-200B jets. When the president of the United States flies in either one, it is designated Air Force One.

UNITED STATES OF AMERICA

What's a supersonic aircraft?

If a friend stands across the room from you and claps her hands, you'll hear the sound almost instantly. It travels so quickly to your ears that it doesn't appear to be moving.

But sound does move, and its speed changes. High above the earth, where the air is very thin, sound travels more slowly than it does near the ground. At 43,000 feet, sound travels at a little less than 700 miles an hour. Planes that can fly faster than sound are called **supersonic.**

The Bell X-I, shown in flight, was powered by four rocket chambers.

SMITHSONIAN LINK
See the actual *Glamorous Glennis* in the National Air and Space Museum's "Milestones of Flight" gallery. Learn more about the Bell X-1 and see it online at: http://www.nasm.si.edu/research/aero/aircraft/bellx1.htm

The Smithsonian's collection includes an early Bell X-1 that was painted orange for easier tracking. Later, it was found that white planes tracked even better.

Pilot Chuck Yeager stands beside his Bell X-1, called *Glamorous Glennis*.

GLAMOROUS GLENNIS

How fast can it fly?

On October 14, 1947, Chuck Yeager was flying at 43,000 feet in a **rocket**-powered plane when he became the first pilot to fly faster than sound. As a plane gets close to the speed of sound, it reaches a point where drag—the air pressure that pushes a plane backward—increases. It's like flying into a wall of air, and the plane shakes and bounces. Early planes sometimes tore apart when pilots tried this. But Yeager kept increasing his speed, and the Bell X-1 was suddenly flying smoothly again at 700 miles per hour—faster than sound.

What do jets do in war?

The German Messerschmitt Me 262 was the first jet used by the military.

A captured German Messerschmitt Me 262 sits on an airfield at the end of World War II, in April 1945.

A B-52 Stratofortress takes off in a cloud of dust and jet exhaust.

The earliest jets could not break the sound barrier, but they were plenty fast. The German Messerschmitt Me 262 could fly at 540 miles per hour, much faster than any of the other planes used in World War II.

The U.S. military scrambled to come up with its own jets. Not long after the war ended, Americans had a brand-new jet bomber, the B-52. The B-52 has wings that carry fuel tanks and have wheels at their tips, to keep the plane balanced as it takes off and lands. Nobody fell in love with this plane for its looks. Its nickname is the BUFF, for "big ugly fat fellow."

But the B-52 turned out to be one of the best planes ever designed. It carries a crew of five or six, and can fly more than 8,000 miles on one tank of fuel. Fifty years after it was first built, the B-52 is still being flown.

The B-52 is a big, heavy airplane. The United States and other countries also needed lighter planes and found one in the F-16 fighter. These quick jets are not as expensive to build as a B-52 and can fly at twice the speed of sound, around 1,350 miles per hour.

Jets are important for the military, but they have other uses as well.

A B-52 can fly up to **650** miles per hour.

Pan American Airlines was one of the first to fly the Boeing 707.

Big, quick, and **powerful**, jets are **perfect** for airliners.

A sleek De Havilland Comet takes a 1951 test flight.

What was the first passenger jet?

After World War II, some jet bombers were used to carry passengers. But these planes were not very comfortable and were so noisy that passengers couldn't hear one another speak. (They wrote notes instead.)

The De Havilland Comet was supposed to change all that. It was the first real passenger jet and also the first plane with a pressurized cabin. This meant that it could fly high (8 miles above Earth), where the air is cold and so thin that people can't breathe it. But the air in the cabin stayed warm. People could breathe and even sleep comfortably.

Comets flew well at first, but as the planes got older, they developed a problem. The metal skin around the planes was so thin that it ripped open, and the planes exploded in flight. Two were lost in 1954, and after that no more Comets flew.

But a new jet was ready to take over. The Boeing 707 was much safer, with a thicker skin that would not break open in flight. The first planes used to fly passengers from New York to Los Angeles, crossing the United States nonstop, were 707s. Soon millions of people every year were flying in jets.

The largest jumbo jet, the Airbus A380, has a wingspan longer than a hockey rink.

What's a jumbo jet?

Airline companies needed big aircraft that could carry all the passengers who wanted to fly. These gigantic planes are called jumbo jets.

The first jumbo jet was the Boeing 747. The Boeing company had to build a special factory big enough to put its 747s together.

What's the fastest passenger jet?

People not only wanted to fly—they wanted to fly *fast*. The Concorde was the first supersonic passenger plane, designed to travel faster than the speed of sound. It flew twice as fast as a 747 could. But the Concorde was expensive to build (each cost $500 million) and fly (it needed almost a ton of fuel for each passenger). Only 16 were ever flown commercially and all of them were grounded in 2003 after nearly 35 years of flight.

The Concorde flew between New York and London in **three** hours.

At its fastest, the Concorde could fly 1,490 miles per hour.

AIR FRANCE

What's a stealth plane? Why is it hard to see?

Jumbo jets are designed to carry lots of people. Fighter jets are designed to be fast and turn quickly. Other jets are designed to be hard to see.

Governments have always wanted to keep an eye on what other countries are doing. Flying is a good way to do this. During the American Civil War, before airplanes were invented, people spied on the other side's army from balloons.

Today, governments use stealth planes to get information. A stealth plane has a quiet engine, so it's hard to hear.

It's painted **black,** so it can't be seen at **night.**

Its flattened shape and a special coating on its surface also make it hard to see on radar. (But rain or hail can cause problems for stealth planes and make it easier for radar to find them.) The SR-71 Blackbird was the United States's first stealth plane. It flies at a record-breaking speed, three times the speed of sound, and soars almost 90,000 feet above the earth, taking pictures of the ground below. The B-2 bomber, another stealth plane with a design called a flying wing, can fly almost 7,000 miles on one tank of fuel—a quarter of the way around the world.

The stealth plane SR-71, called the Blackbird, can fly 17 miles above the earth.

SMITHSONIAN LINK
Find any aircraft that is part of the National Air and Space Museum's collection, including the Lockheed SR-71 Blackbird, at:
http://www.nasm.si.edu/research/aero/aircraft/

What takes off like a rocket and lands like an airplane?

Since the Wright brothers' first flight (about 15 feet off the ground) people have been building planes to go higher and higher. Highest of all, of course, is a plane that can travel into space.

The space shuttle blasts off like a rocket. In fact, it uses two booster rockets to help it escape Earth's gravity. These rockets fall off, and the shuttle orbits alone, 250 miles above Earth. When it returns, it lands like an airplane—actually, like a glider. The space shuttle doesn't use any power of its own as it comes in for a landing, which makes it a bit like the early aircraft made by Cayley or Lilienthal.

The Ansari X Prize is a $10 million reward for the first spaceship *not* built by a government to reach 63 miles above Earth, a height that is called **suborbital space.** SpaceShipOne won the prize in 2004. Like the shuttle, SpaceShipOne is a little like a rocket and a little like an airplane. It was carried up to 47,000 feet by another plane, and then it blasted away on its own, rocketing up to 71.5 miles above Earth for a few minutes. Afterward it glided down for a landing much as the space shuttle does.

SMITHSONIAN LINK
Check out the space shuttle *Enterprise*
via a live webcam at:
http://www.nasm.si.edu/interact/webcams/

The space shuttle belongs to the United States, but not all spaceships are owned by governments.

A space shuttle orbits Earth with its cargo bay doors open to space.

A wide-angle view of a space shuttle's cockpit shows the many blue display screens and hundreds of lighted switches and controls that the crew uses to fly the spacecraft.

What will new kinds of spaceships look like?

Ordinary people may one day be able to buy a ticket for a trip into space as easily as they buy a ticket for an airplane today.

A few very rich people have already gone into space as tourists. Dennis Tito paid $20 million for a trip to the International Space Station. Others have followed.

Some people think that ordinary tourists may be able to travel into space in as little as 5 or 10 years. It may take longer. Nobody knows for sure.

We also don't know what the aircraft of the future will look like.

Will they have wings like an airplane to let them glide down for a landing? Will they take off like a rocket, straight up into the sky? Maybe ships will be built that never come down to Earth at all but leave and return from space stations orbiting the planet.

It's hard to imagine what tomorrow's aircraft will look like. But we do know that human beings won't stay on the ground. We love to fly, and we will always be looking for ways to travel into the sky or to reach new worlds in outer space.

SMITHSONIAN LINK
See the actual SpaceShipOne in the National Air and Space Museum's "Milestones of Flight" gallery. Learn all about the SpaceShipOne and see it online at: http://www.nasm.si.edu/exhibitions/gal100/ss1.htm

SpaceShipOne hangs beneath the jet aircraft called *White Knight*, which carries it high in the air before releasing the rocket for a trip into space.

Space tourist Dennis Tito floats through the International Space Station high above Earth.

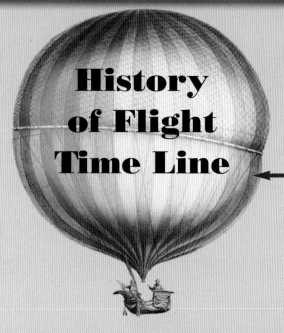

History of Flight Time Line

1300s: Explorer Marco Polo sees kites carrying people in China.

1500s: Leonardo da Vinci sketches plans for flying machines.

1783: Humans first fly in a hot-air balloon, invented by the Montgolfier brothers of France.

1804–1853: Sir George Cayley of England experiments with gliders.

1852: First powered airship, made by Henri Giffard of France, flies.

1903: Orville Wright makes first powered, heavier-than-air human flight.

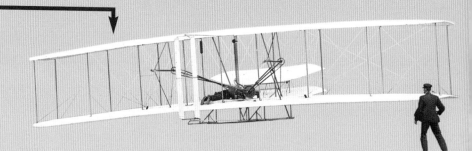

1908: Thérèse Peltier becomes the first woman to fly as a passenger.

1915: First successful fighter plane, the German Fokker Eindecker, is used in combat.

1917: The British Sopwith Camel fighter plane is first used in combat. It shoots down more enemy planes than any other plane in World War I.

1926: Ford introduces the Tri-Motor for passenger flight.

1927: Charles Lindbergh makes the first nonstop solo flight across the Atlantic Ocean (in 33½ hours).

1932: Amelia Earhart becomes the first woman to fly solo across the Atlantic Ocean.

1933: First modern airliner, Boeing 247, is launched.

1933: Wiley Post becomes the first pilot to fly alone around the world (in 7 days, 9 hours).

1936: Douglas DC-3 makes its first commercial flight.

1937: German airship the *Hindenburg* explodes and crashes in New Jersey.

1938: Boeing 314 Clipper flying boat is launched.

1939: Russian-born U.S. citizen Igor Sikorsky invents the first successful helicopter.

1944: German Messerschmitt Me 262, the first jet fighter, flies in combat.

1947: Charles Yeager becomes the first pilot to fly faster than the speed of sound.

1949: Test flight made of the first jet airliner, the British De Havilland Comet.

1954: Boeing 707 makes first flight.

1961 (April 12)**:** Yuri Gagarin of the Soviet Union becomes the first human in space.

1961 (May 5)**:** Alan Shepard becomes the first American in space.

1962: Lockheed SR-71 Blackbird stealth plane makes its first flight.

1976: The Concorde supersonic jet makes its first commercial flight between New York and London.

1981: First space shuttle, the *Columbia*, flies.

1989: B-2 stealth bomber makes its first flight.

2004: SpaceShipOne, the first privately built spaceship to reach suborbital space, wins the Ansari X Prize.

Why did you become a historian?

In college, I thought I wanted to be a scientist because I wanted to help develop alternative energy sources. But, by my senior year, I realized that I was more interested in learning about why we use so much energy and why we seemed to always want to go faster, farther, and higher. Studying history seemed a better course for exploring the answers to my questions.

What incident or person from your childhood influenced your decision?

Science and history seem to be intertwined throughout my life. When I was in second grade, I was invited to study geology (the history of the earth) with the sixth grade class. To look at rock formations for ourselves, we scrambled up and down the angled limestone walls surrounding the school playground. The vinegar we dropped on the rock fizzed, and our magnifying glasses revealed the hard edges of millions of fossilized plants and animals—it was amazing. From that point on, I think I always was interested in learning about how things came to be and how we learned about the past.

How can kids get interested in your field?

Look around you. History is everywhere. If you like a particular sport, for example, write down everything you know about your sport and how you learned it, and make an argument for why you think that sport is important or interesting. You just have to start investigating something that interests you.

What do you do every day?

One of the best features of working as a museum curator is that every day is unique. Sometimes I spend the entire day searching through historical documents looking for information about a subject. Other days I look for photographs to illustrate a book, participate in a discussion about creating a new exhibition, write labels, or organize objects in the museum's collection.

Where do you do your research?

I surf the Internet at my desk in my office at the museum and take trips to the National Archives, the Library of Congress, the Smithsonian Archives, and many other places to do research.

What are the most important qualities for an expert in your field?

I think the most important qualities are curiosity, persistence, and an interest in people today and in the past.

What new technology has helped you most with your job?

The Internet has greatly influenced my approach to researching new topics.

What are some of the most unusual objects in the Smithsonian collection you work with?

I am responsible for curating—recording the objects in the NASM poster collection, ensuring that they are stored properly, learning about the objects' history, and creating a strategy to enhance the collection by collecting new objects. I think the posters are intriguing because they help tell a unique story in aviation history—how aviation promoters, from balloon exhibition sponsors to airlines, sold aviation to the public.

What skills and tools do you need to do your job?

To do my job, you need many of the skills you would need to be a detective. You need to be able to learn about new topics, determine what facts are worthwhile and which sources should be discounted, and convey an argument clearly and engagingly to an audience.

What keeps you doing what you do?

Although I have sat through many classes to earn my degrees, I think that I would have enjoyed the learning process

more if I had had the opportunity to learn in a practical setting—like the museum. I hope that my work at the NASM teaches visitors to think about the objects surrounding us every day as portals to stories about history, science, politics. Most of all, I hope that my work encourages museum visitors to think about questions such as: Why do we collect objects in the first place? What makes an object valuable? What is value? I hope my work starts that conversation.

Glossary

airplane—an aircraft with wings that is heavier than air and can fly under its own power

cargo—anything (except people) being transported from place to place. Planes have carried cargo such as food, medicine, and mail, and almost anything else you can imagine.

drag—the force created when air pushes against a moving object, slowing it down

Dunkirk—a town on the coast of northern France from which thousands of British, French, and Belgium troops were forced to retreat to England from the German army in 1940

glider—an aircraft with wings that floats on the wind but cannot move under its own power; similar to an airplane, but without an engine

gravity—the force that attracts or pulls objects together

hydrogen—the lightest of all gases, it has no color and no odor and burns very easily

jet fuel—the liquid that is burned inside a jet engine; may be kerosene or a mixture of kerosene, gasoline, and other liquids

Leonardo da Vinci—one of the most famous painters and inventors in the world, lived from 1452 to 1519

lift—the force created when air pressure below a surface is greater than air pressure above it

propeller—a device with two or more blades that can turn very quickly. When a propeller on the nose of an airplane or airship turns, it pulls the craft forward through the air.

rocket—an engine that carries its own supply of air or oxygen so it can burn fuel even in space where there is no air. Jet engines use the outside air to burn fuel, so jets don't work in space.

suborbital space—sixty-three miles above Earth. Astronauts in suborbital space experience weightlessness but are not moving fast enough to orbit Earth.

supersonic—faster than the speed of sound. The speed of sound changes depending on how high something is above the earth, so "supersonic" can refer to many different actual speeds.

thrust—the force that moves an object forward

More to See and Read

Websites

There are links to many wonderful web pages in this book. But the web is constantly growing and changing and we cannot guarantee that the sites we recommend will be available. If the site you want is no longer there, you can always find your way to plenty of information about the aircraft and a great learning experience through the main Smithsonian website: www.si.edu.

Visit the site of the Smithsonian National Air and Space Museum to find information about and pictures of the Wright Flyer, the British Spitfire, the SR-71 Blackbird, the space shuttle *Enterprise*, and many more historic aircraft. www.nasm.si.edu/

Discover activities, information, and projects about airplanes, rockets, and the space shuttle here. www.nasa.gov/audience/forkids/home/index.html

Find out more about SpaceShipOne and see photos and videos here. www.scaled.com/projects/tierone/

Suggested Reading

Flying Machine (Eyewitness Books)

Wings and Rockets: The Story of Women in Air and Space, by Jeannine Atkins, illustrated by Dušan Petričič

Fantastic Flights: One Hundred Years of Flying on the Edge, by Patrick O'Brien

My Brothers' Flying Machine: Wilbur, Orville, and Me, by Jane Yolen, illustrated by Jim Burke

Feathers, Flaps, and Flops: Fabulous Early Fliers, by Bo Zaunders, illustrated by Roxie Munro

Index